Realpolitik:
Han Fei on mighty reign

Translated by Mingyuan Hu

Hermits United
London · Paris

Published in Great Britain by Hermits United Ltd. 2023
English translation copyright © Mingyuan Hu 2023
Printed in Europe

This book is part of the Erstwhile Series
A catalogue record for this book is available
from the British Library
ISBN 978-1-7391156-3-0

www.hermits-united.com

Realpolitik

280–233 BC

Variously considered a Taoist and a cynic, Han Fei, himself a prince, has been seen as a forerunner to Machiavelli. At the end of the Warring States, when oratory mattered hugely, Han Fei, with a stutter, was the brain and the plume of the Legalist School. From Han Fei's oeuvre, Mingyuan Hu selects and translates two extracts encapsulating the thinking that so seduced Zheng, King of Qin, who later became the first emperor of China, and in whose prison Han Fei died drinking poison.

仁義用於古、不用於今也　　　11

Goodness and Honour　　　20
Are for Ancient Times,
Not for Today

救小未必能存、而交大未必不有疏　　38

Rescuing a Small Power　　41
May Not Help Its Survival;
Serving the Powerful
May Not Be Free of Oversight

仁義用於古、不用於今也

上古之世、人民少而禽獸眾、人民不勝禽獸蟲蛇。有聖人作、構木為巢以避群害、而民悅之、使王天下、號之曰有巢氏。民食果蓏蚌蛤、腥臊惡臭而傷害腹胃、民多疾病。有聖人作、鑽燧取火以化腥臊、而民說之、使王天下、號之曰燧人氏。中古之世、天下大水、而鯀、禹決瀆。近古之世、桀、紂暴亂、而湯、武征伐。今有構木鑽燧於夏后氏之世者、必為鯀、禹笑矣。有決瀆於殷、周之世者、必為湯、武笑矣。然則今有美堯、舜、鯀、禹、湯、武之道於當今之世者、必為新聖笑矣。是以聖人不期修古、不法常可、論世之事、因為之備。宋人有耕者、田中有株、兔走觸株、折頸而死。因釋其耒而守株、冀復得兔。兔不可復得，而身為宋國笑。今欲以先王之政、治當世之民、皆守株之類也。古者丈夫不耕、草木之實足食也。婦人不織、禽獸之皮足衣也。不事力而養足、人民少而財有餘、故民不爭。

是以厚賞不行、重罰不用、而民自治。今人有五子不為多、子又有五子、大父未死而有二十五孫。是以人民眾而貨財寡、事力勞而供養薄、故民爭、雖倍賞累罰而不免於亂。堯之王天下也、茅茨不翦、采椽不斲、糲粢之食、藜藿之羹、冬日麑裘、夏日葛衣、雖監門之服養、不虧於此矣。禹之王天下也、身執耒臿以為民先、股無完胈、脛不生毛、雖臣虜之勞、不苦於此矣。以是言之、夫古之讓天子者、是去監門之養而離臣虜之勞也、古傳天下而不足多也。今之縣令、一日身死、子孫累世絜駕、故人重之。是以人之於讓也、輕辭古之天子、難去今之縣令者、薄厚之實異也。夫山居而谷汲者、膢臘而相遺以水。澤居苦水者、買庸而決竇。故饑歲之春、幼弟不饟。穰歲之秋、疏客必食。非疏骨肉愛過客也、多少之實異也。是以古之易財、非仁也、財多也。今之爭奪、非鄙也、財寡也。輕辭天子、非高也、勢薄也。爭士橐、非下也、權重也。故聖人議多少、論薄厚為之政。故罰薄不為慈、誅嚴不為戾、稱俗而行也。故事因於世、而備適於事。古者文王處豐、鎬之間、地方百里、行仁義而懷西戎、遂王天下。徐偃王處漢東、地方五百里、行仁義、割地而朝者三十有六國。荊文王恐其害己也、舉兵伐徐、遂滅之。故文王行仁義而王天下、偃王行仁義而喪其國、是仁義用於古、不用於今也。故曰、世異則事異。當舜之時、有苗不服、禹將伐之。舜曰、不可。上德不厚而行武、非道也。乃修教三年、執干戚舞、有苗乃服。共工之戰、鐵銛矩者及乎敵、鎧甲不堅者傷乎體、是干戚用於古不用於今也。故曰、事異則備變。上古競于道德、中世逐於智謀、當今爭於氣力。齊將攻魯、魯使子貢說之。齊人曰、子言非不辯也、吾所欲者土地也、非斯言所謂也。遂舉兵伐魯、去門十里以為界。故偃王仁義而徐亡、子貢辯智而魯削。以是言之、夫仁義辯智、非所以持國也。去偃王之仁、息子貢之智、循徐、魯之力使敵萬乘、則齊、荊之欲不得行於二國矣。夫古今異俗、新故異備。如欲以寬緩之政、治急世之民、猶無轡策而御駻馬、此不知之患也。今儒、墨皆稱先王兼愛天下、則視民如父母。何以明其然也。曰、司寇行刑、君為之不舉樂、聞死刑之報、君為流涕。此所舉先王也。夫以君臣為如父子則必治、推是言之、是無亂父子也。人之情性、莫先於父母、皆見愛而未必治也、雖厚愛矣、奚遽不亂。今先王之愛民、不過父母之愛子、子未必不亂也、則民奚遽治哉。且夫以法行刑而君為之流涕、此以效仁、非以為治也。夫垂泣不欲刑者、仁也。然而不可不刑者、法也。先王勝其法、不聽其泣、則仁之不可以為治亦明矣。

Goodness and Honour Are for Ancient Times, Not for Today

In early antiquity, men were few and animals many; humans could not compete with beasts. A sage made nests sheltering his kind. Delighted, the people made him king, naming him He Who Makes Nests. Eating raw fruits and rancid clams, people had troubled intestines. A sage produced fire to cook food. Delighted, the people made him king, naming him He Who Produces Fire. In mid-antiquity, deluge was everywhere;

Gun and Yu diverted rivers. Later, Jie and Zhou ruled with violence; against them Tang and Wu waged wars. If, by the time of Xia, one made nests and fire, Gun and Yu would have laughed. If, by the time of Yin and Zhou, one diverted rivers, Tang and Wu would have laughed. If today one admired and practised the ways of Yao, Shun, Gun, Yu, Tang and Wu, today's sages would have laughed. So the sage mimics not the old, nor follows the settled. He discerns the present reality, and devises policies accordingly.

There once was a farmer from Song. In his field was a tree, into which one day a rabbit ran, broke its neck and died. The farmer thence abandoned his plough and waited by the tree for rabbits. No other rabbit ever arrived, and the man was ridiculed by all. Now, if one used older kings' politics to govern today's populace, one would be waiting by the tree.

In ancient times men did not till the soil, wild vegetation being enough for eating; women did not weave, animal skin being enough for wearing; people did not labour and supplies were sufficient; the population was small and assets were adequate. For that reason, people did not fight one another. With no lavish rewards nor severe punishments, they remained law-abiding citizens. Nowadays, a man has at least five children, each of which has at least five of their own. Not yet dead, one is a grandfather of twenty-five. So the population is large and assets are scarce; people labour and the pay is meagre. For that reason, people fight one another. Even with rewards doubled and punishments multiplied, chaos may not be avoided.

When Yao was King of all, he lived in an unadorned hut, ate

unrefined food, wore a piece of deer fur in winter and a slash of rough cloth in summer: the conditions of a warden today are no meaner. When Yu was King of all, he carried ploughs and spades and led people in the fields, his thighs thinned from fatigue, hair rubbed off his shins: the chores of a servant today are no rougher. Speaking in such terms, when kings of old abdicated, they were rid of a warden's conditions and a servant's chores, such being not much of a loss; when a provincial governor of our day dies, generations of his offspring have horse chariots, such being a prized allowance. Therefore, renouncing kingship in the old days was effortless and renouncing provincial functions today strenuous, for there is a real difference in what there is to lose. Now, hill people fetching water from the valley gift one another with water; lowlanders suffering from floods hire help to dig ditches for drainage. In years of bad harvest, one feeds not one's younger brother; in years of good harvest, one invites visitors to supper. Not that one alienates family and favours guests, but there is a real difference in how much one can spare. The ancients took assets lightly, not because they were admirable but because assets were plenty. Today's men fight over capital, not because they are despicable but because capital is wanting. Ancient kings resigned readily, not because they were lofty but because the stakes of power were low. Today's men compete for office, not because they are base but because the benefits are prodigious. Ergo, the sage devises policies according to the capital and power in question. Light penalties imply not benevolence and heavy penance not viciousness, for they befit society's needs. Matters are conditioned by the times, and measures serve present reality.

In ancient times, King Wen of Zhou had a territory of a hundred *li*. Exercising goodness and honour, he impressed the neighbouring peoples and became king of all. Latterly, King Yan of Xu had a territory of five hundred *li*. Exercising goodness and honour, he had thirty-six states offering him land and pledging allegiance. Fearful of being imperilled, King Wen of Chu invaded and ravaged Xu. So, with goodness and honour, King Wen of Zhou became king of all; with goodness and honour, King Yan of Xu lost his realm, because goodness and honour are for ancient times, not for today. As they say: matters change with the times.

When Shun was king, the Miao people were defiant. Yu suggested subduing them by force. Shun said: 'No. Employing force before exerting morality does not conform to the Tao.' He then spent three years enforcing ethical education, teaching dance with shields and axes until the Miao were subdued. Came the War of Gonggong, short weapons and feeble armours left soldiers exposed and wounded, for the ancient dance of shields and axes was of no use. As they say: measures change with present reality.

In early antiquity, what counted was morality. In mid-antiquity, what counted was strategy. Today, what counts is force. When Qi prepared to attack Lu, Lu sent Zigong to dissuade Qi. Qi said to Zigong: 'What you say, Sir, is quite wise. What I want however is lands, not your sagesse.' Qi attacked, and conquered most of Lu's land. So, King Yan practised goodness and Xu was demolished; Zigong exercised intellect and Lu was diminished. Goodness and intellect cannot protect a state. Dispense with King Yan's goodness and do without Zigong's intellect, and build Xu and Lu's military might against enemies of a thousand chariots: in this way, the two states might have survived Qi and Chu's attack.

As customs change, rules change. Ruling a disgruntled people in desperate times with benign policies is like harnessing wild horses without bridles or whips; it leads to unwitting calamities. Today, both Confucianists and Mohists claim that ancient kings comported themselves as loving parents to the people. How do they know? 'When an execution was underway', they say, 'the sovereign stopped playing music. The execution being reported, he was moved to tears.' This is the ancient king they praised. Now, if a father-son rapport between a king and his people ensured good governance, we would conceive of no trouble between fathers and sons. Yet, parental love being supreme, even with this love, not all families are at peace. The sovereign can indeed love his subjects. Yet, A king's love being inferior to a parent's, seeing children go against their parents, do people not go against kingly rule? Grieving over an execution evinces the sovereign's goodness, which is of no use to governance.

Wishing not to execute criminals out of compassion, this is good. Going ahead with the execution, that is law. The ancient king upheld law despite his compassion. Clearly, goodness can be of no use to governance.

救小未必能存、而交大未必不有疏

故群臣之言外事者、非有分於從衡之黨、則有仇讎之忠、而借力於國也。從者、合眾弱以攻一強也。而衡者、事一強以攻眾弱也。皆非所以持國也。今人臣之言衡者、皆曰、不事大、則遇敵受禍矣。事大未必有實、則舉圖而委、效璽而請兵矣。獻圖則地削、效璽則名卑、地削則國削、名卑則政亂矣。事大為衡未見其利也、而亡地亂政矣。人臣之言從者、皆曰、不救小而伐大、則失天下、失天下則國危、國危而主卑。救小未必有實、則起兵而敵大矣。救小未必能存、而交大未必不有疏、有疏則為強國制矣。出兵則軍敗、退守則城拔。救小為從未見其利、而亡地敗軍矣。

Rescuing a Small Power
May Not Help Its Survival;
Serving the Powerful
May Not Be Free of Oversight

Those who speak of foreign affairs, be they of Vertical or Horizontal Alliance, do so for personal vengeance and not in their countries' interest. Vertical Alliance unites small powers against a great one. Horizontal Alliance sides with a great power against smaller ones. Neither protects a state.

Those for Horizontal Alliance say: 'Not serving a great power, we will suffer at the hands of enemies.' While serving the powerful may not entail real action, one already gives away sovereignty in exchange for protection. With this, the territory is diminished and the country humbled. Before this Horizontal Alliance siding with the great sees benefit, the land is compromised and domestic politics becoming turbulent.

Those for Vertical Alliance say: 'Not coming to a small power's rescue nor confronting the great, we will lose the esteem of all.

Our country will be jeopardised and our sovereign humbled.' While saving the small may not entail real action, with troops mobilised, one is already enemies with the great. Rescuing a small power may not help its survival, no more than serving the powerful may be free of oversight, subjecting one to its sway. Sending troops, one's troops will lose. Withdrawing, one's own cities will fall. Before this Vertical Alliance backing the small sees benefit, one's land is compromised and one's army vanquished.